EVACUEE
A WARTIME CHILDHOOD

BRIAN SANDERS

SMALL
FORT

My first memory is of a very beautiful pigeon that came to our window-sill to be fed. His neck shimmered with purple and green. Although his tail was only grey, he was very proud of it.

Then there was a silver sausage with ears and high in the sky were lots of crosses with puffy white patterns against the blue. Sometimes a cross would fall down with black smoke chasing it. Daddy made a cross for me. I think that I was three.

And then it was dark, but the sky was all lit up. Mum said — "Please don't go out love", but Daddy said "Have to help, be back soon" and in the morning he came home all dirty.

Then he went to fight the war. Mum cried

We went to a place called Somerset to collect my sister Sylvie who had been sent there to get away from the **BOMBS**
There were lots of ducks on a pond and cows in a field.
The farmer and his wife were very kind but we did not stay long.

We went back by train to LONDON.

We collected our belongings which Mum said would be packed
in boxes until we could find somewhere else to live.

Then we all went on another train from a smokey old station out **to the** country

but I must have fallen asleep

'cos when I woke up I was **in a cage.......**

.. but it was only an indoor shelter where the children of Mum's friend slept in c of air raids. We all played together unt breakfast tim

Mum soon found us rooms in a big old house. My bedroom was on the top floor.

She did our washing in an outside wash-house in the yard. Sylvie helped her.

Our living room was also the kitchen. It had no water, so it all had to be carried upstairs and heated on the gas stove in kettles and pots.

On bath nights it was not very easy for Mum who had been at work all day and then had to make us supper and light the fire. The coal also had to be brought up by hand.

Mum did war work - Sylvie
went to school, so I was
looked after by Tredgett who I loved.
She called me boy Brian and
Sylvie gal Syly, her wackee wees, which was
her way of saying evacuees.

Tredgett and Mrs Scruby, who lived next door, were good
friends. They called each other Scruby and Tredgett
I called her Mrs Scruby. Her daughter was one of the
children I played with in the yard. When I was
older I played with the
big boys.

Tredgett's house was in the yard of a small holding, which is not quite as big as
a farm. The owner was called Uncle Arthur. He had a lorry, a tractor, a horse
a cart and kept pigs. He also had lots of grandchildren who lived nearby and
played in the yard. The barns and bushes were great for hide and seek.

Tredgett cooked over the fire and in its oven. My place was between her chair and the cubby hole. With the barley tin on a tray it could be a railway engine or sometimes a spitfire. Mr Tredgett was very old and wore gaiters over his boots. He did not have to go to the war this time.

e thought flowers were waste of space nd dug for victory on the loppa. e was at war with

At the top end of the loppa was the orchard where I helped feed the chickens and their chicks.

We collected eggs each day. Sometimes, if a hen was broody, we had to feel underneath her to find the eggs and she would get cross.

We also kept rabbits. They sometimes went to visit their relatives,

but did not come back again. I wondered why.

Tredgett taught me how to find good things to eat like mushrooms and how to tell if they were poisonous. We collected blackberries from the hedgerows. May bushes were called bread and cheese because you could eat their leaves and berries. The leaves tasted better in the Spring. We picked little wild strawberries at the edge of the wood. They were sweet.

Because we were near to the aerodrome we saw lots of planes. Sometimes they wiggled their wings when we waved.

The old car covered with sandbags was a shelter in case a "Gerry" plane came over.

Carthorse Charlotte and I became friends. She liked apples and I gave her windfalls. Sometimes Uncle Arthur took me with him to deliver flower in powdery sacks. The baker gave me a hot roll straight from the oven. Bread was not rationed but nearly all food was, so we were often hungry. The roll smelled and tasted heaven

On summer nights Charlotte slept in the Plantation. I loved to ride her there. Uncle Arthur and his daughter Vera helped me. Sylvie came to Tredgett's after school and Mum collected us after work. Then we walked (I trotted) home to the other end of town. Every night before bed we said our prayers, always ending God bless Daddy and keep him SAFE.

Three other people shared the house because there was a war on. Aunt Lal who had big teeth, her husband Charlie and Miss Saker. She had a fox fur and a handbag made from a crocodile. I think she liked animals. They were all kind to me, but Sylvie did not like Aunt Lal. She always put silver thrupenny bits into her Christmas puddings. I found one, so did Lal, but Sylvie wasn't so lucky.

I caught scarlet fever and was put in the ISOLATION HOSPITAL. Tredgett came to talk to me across the ditch around Uncle Arthur's field, but a nurse scolded us and took me inside.

When I could not stop crying 'cos I missed Tredgett, she put me in the bath and =SLAPPED ME=

A kind airman rescued me and took me to Matron who gave me a sweet. The airman said he had children himself. I wasn't smacked any more.

When I was four and a half I went to school with Sylvie. She did not enjoy that as she was five years older and I dawdled. I was an infant.

We had to carry our gas masks with us in their brown cardboard boxes. Mine was called a Micky Mouse, but it did not look like him. Its nose wiggled when you breathed. Sylvie's was the same as a grown up's.

When the air raid siren sounded you got ready to put on your gas mask

Pistol

Tommy Gun

Fighter 'Plane

Our teachers were all women and forbad toy guns at school - but we did not need them!

Bomber

School was fun. We had a wood box. I made a big battle ship with lots of nails. We also had a claybin.

We built a shop by collecting used tins and boxes. Miss found us some cardboard money with play ten shilling and pound notes.

Students from the teacher training college next to our school said they would take us fishing on Saturday if the weather stayed fine. Ella and Dot, Tredgett's daughters, made me a rod from a blackthorn stick. It had screw eyes and a cotton reel winder. I worried that it would rain, but Tredgett said "if there was enough blue in the sky to patch an old man's trousers it wouldn't." There was and it didn't. We caught lots of creatures. One was a stickleback who ate my worm and would not let go, but I set him free because he was so pretty. A few weeks later we went to the college to see something else that we had caught turn into something else. It began like this. and ended as a dragon fly. It is called METAMORPHOSIS.

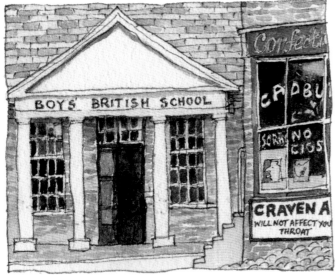

When I was five and a half I went to big boy's school. There was a shop opposite that did not have much to sell, BECAUSE THERE WAS A WAR ON and sweets were rationed even if there were any. All of our teachers were women except for our headmaster who was a very kind man. He did not have to go to fight the war.

We learned lots of history visiting the town's museum and saw Saxon skeletons found in the battle ditches.

Going to the ruins of the Norman castle keep we looked at the stocks, but did not go in because it was probably haunted by people who had been tortured and it was dangerous because stones kept falling off.

The museum also had lots of stuffed animals and birds in glass cases

Miss taught us how to make Norman helmets, shields, swords, bows, arrows and sheaths to hold them. The Saxons had jerkins, helmets and daggers.

Saxon

Norman

Winter sledge run

The Maze

all went onto the Common, which was our playground, for a battle. Guess who won? ...old pretended to have an arrow in his eye. Miss took a picture of us.

...hese were my toys. I kept most of them in a shoebox. Sylvie made Peter Rabbit for me.

...th my penknife I made a Three Musketeers ...pier by punching a hole in a tin lid and ...ushing a stick through it. The ...ark was left on the handle and the ...row heads to help them to fire ...raight. Lime tree withies were the straightest sticks.

Some Sundays Mum took us for a walk across the Park to the Mansion. We could not go int
it because of the soldiers and there being a war on. As it was very secret, we did not kno
that the manhole in the bridge hid lots of dynamite to be blown up if the
Germans invaded. We also only learned after the war how brave the men and
women soldiers at the house were. They came from Poland and were parachute
back there to fight the Germans who had occupied their country. There is now a
memorial to those who lost their lives. It is near to the Lion Gate.

This was the year that the Americans came.
Some did not like being called Yanks because
they came from the Southern States. Mum did
not let us ask "got any gum chum?" She said it
was begging. But often you did not have to
ask, they just gave it to you anyway.

One G.I. gave me a box of candy
for Mum. She made me take it
back. I was very sad. It looked
like more than a year's sweet ratio

I thought  was delicious

At Christmas they collected us in one of ir trucks and took us to their base for a

Wonderful Party

I had my first ice-cream and Henry wore a real flying helmet.

As there was not much to sell some shops made patriotic displays in their windows. The models were spiffing, the planes very realistic and I wanted one. Mum said she would try to get me one for Christmas. When I opened my present it was a big disappointment, but I did not let Mum know. It had all sharp edges and nothing had been rounded off.

Because it was made by a German prisoner of war, it was a

STUKA

so later we shot it down, just like they did Peter's Dad.

Across the road from where we lived and next to the pub was the gate to a secret garden was our playground. At one end was a viewing platform you could pretend was anything from a bomber to a pirate ship. There were lots and lots of places to play hide and seek. Its pond was home to newts and frogs. The garden is still there and anyone can go in, but don't get lost in the hedge maze which is much better than the one at Hampton Court and much harder to find your way out of.

Drawing and painting was what I liked doing most of all. If Sylvie wanted me to be quiet she bribed me with sheets of paper, which had to have no lines. I always wanted to be an artist and I'm still trying.

Miss pinned this one I did of a Roman soldier on the wall. The big red sun was done with a lovely soft pastel crayon. I was sad when it was all used up.

Mum wrote to Daddy a lot at night after she'd put her curlers in. Sometimes, if it wasn't on a forces airmail for she sent one of my drawings

The funny basket was made from ropes of coloured raffia and inside were oranges beautifully wrapped in pretty tissue papers with pictures printed on them. We hardly ever had an orange BECAUSE THERE WAS A WAR ON and I tasted my first banana when I was eight.

As we unwrapped the tissues, we found some oranges were also wrapped in big white £5 notes. The sailor said Daddy was very good at cards.

One Sunday when Mum was doing the house work a sailor friend of Daddy's came all the way from North Africa with a strange looking present. Mum was embarrassed because she was in her overalls.

We all had new clothes, or as many as our clothing coupons allowed.

Silk stockings were hard to find and needed lots of coupons and because Mum did not have an American boyfriend, there were no nylons either. She used leg make up instead and as I had a good eye et me draw the lines down the backs f her legs to look like stocking seams nd darken her heels with my brush.

When I was little I cried when Mum went out in the evening, but Sylvie gave me paper without lines so I soon stopped. Mum always went with her friend Ann as there was safety in numbers.

Ann's son Ronnie was in my class at school. Sometimes we went to his house for a proper bath. We could only have five inches of water because there WAS A WAR ON. Ronnie had two boats, one of them clockwork, but his Dad wasn't coming home after the war ended.

Peter was allowed to use his Dad's tools as he would not be coming back from the war. We used them to build a racing cart from wooden boxes and wheels from an old pram. Peter's Grandad helped us with the sawing and bending the metal bits. He also found us the screws and bolts.

When it was finished we tried to race some Americans down Windmill Hill. We did not win, but they threw us some ⁼GUM⁼ not just a stick, but a whole packet.

We liked the Americans especially for their comics which had very shiny covers and were all in colour.

We swapped them with each other. Boys with grown up sisters had the best collections.

If you put your mack over your shoulders and did the top button up rolled your trousers up and your socks down, you could be

SUPERMAN

Mum had a telegram from Granny saying "COME
OON FATHER ILL" Grandfather had been gassed
n the last war and did not get better. Sylvie
tayed with a friend, but Tredgett was ill, so I
vent with Mum to London. We travelled
n the tube. I found a big chocolate
machine but it was empty. I expect you
can guess why.

Mum went to the hospital while Granny
looked after me. She had lilies of the valley
in her window box and put her tea leaves
on them. She liked mild beer putting a
red hot poker into it to warm it up. She
did not go down the Tube at night to avoid
the bombs. She said it was better to be at
home and not get trapped underground.
She had a shawl and wore black clothes
with button boots. We had another
Granny and Grandfather. I will tell you
about them later.

Out the back was an Anderson shelter or
dugout – a hole in the ground covered in
corrugated iron and sandbags. It had two ledges
for sleeping on and a sack to cover the doorway.
Granny did not like it. It was too damp for her old bones and smelled of mold which is
what she called earth. That night Gerry came over, so we all crawled into the cupboard
under the stairs. We took our shoes off because of the mattress on the floor, but kept our
clothes on just in case. There was lots of whistling and big bangs from the bombs. Granny said
"Please God don't let them fall on us." The next day we went home very early,

So I did not see much of London.

Sylvie went to the Grammar School, catching a train every day, but still came to collect me from Tredgett's in the afternoon. We always looked over the railway bridge on the way home. There were more and more tanks and big guns covered with camouflage nets in the sidings and coal yard.

At bedtime the night before MY SEVENTH BIRTHDAY the side of the street leading to the south was teeming with soldiers and all sorts of vehicles. Lorries, tanks, bren gun carriers jeeps, strange things that looked like boats, but had wheels and despatch riders on their motor bikes. They all seemed to be waiting for something to happen.

IT TOOK ME AGES TO GET TO SLEEP I WAS SO EXCITED!

Waking up at first light, which is very early on June 6th, I saw the pair of boys size 6 football boots, that had vanished from De Barrs shoe shop window the week before, were hanging at the end of the bed. It was then that I knew prayers could be answered and my Daddy would come home.

Hanging the boots round my neck just in case they vanished again, I opened the window to see if the fledgling house martins under the eaves had left their nest, but instead saw the sky full of planes towing gliders towards the sun. It was -: D-DAY :-

The street was empty - the soldiers all gone

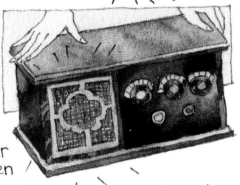

After breakfast and wishing me a happy birthday, Mum went to work, Sylvie and me to school. Teacher brought in her accumulator radio for us to listen to the news, but we were all too excited to sit still, so she sent us out to play on the common.

We took the bridge over the Slade ....

....Captured a Gerry Gun emplacement – consolidated and took up defensive positions in the turf-maze against counter attack...until milk time.

Gliders and other planes were in the sky all day and even after bedtime

Mum and Dot Tredgett talked to each other a lot because Daddy and Dot's husband Joe were both in the Eighth Army, first in North Africa and now fighting in Italy. They thought that their husbands (and my Daddy) had been forgotten about since D-Day.

They said the blitz was over, so Mum took us on holiday to London to see our other Granny and Grandfather. Mum did not come up with us or stay. I only found out why after the war, but that will be in another book.

From the moment I met them, I loved Granny and Grandfather.

Granny let me pump the hot water from the copper in the kitchen into the bath at bathtime, as there was only a cold water tap in the bathroom.

After the bath she was making us bread and milk - she held the loaf under her arm to cut it -

WHEN!

suddenly the siren at the police station

sounded the air raid warning

Grandfather said, "Somebody has got it wrong".

We heard a funny noise in the sky. A cross between a motorbike and an aeroplane. It stopped and then

there was **A HUGE BANG** and all the windows rattled, and then anothe and fire engine bells. We did not know then, but the first VI doodlebugs had arrive

It was too late to go down the shelter so Granny put us under the table to look after birdie until the "all clear" sounded. Mum soon came and very early next day we went home again. This time we went by bus to the railway station, so were able to see what Gerry had

been up to. Mum said "Londoners will carry on as usual". We learned after the war that the doodlebugs and buzz bombs were all aimed at Tower Bridge which Granny and Grandfather lived very close to.

The war went on. I joined the cubs. Mum dyed me a square of old sheet a lovely blue for my scarf and Sylvie plaited me a woggle from string, but there were no cub caps because of there being a war on. I also joined the choir and sometime after evensong it was dark. As there was a blackout we had torches. You were not allowed to point at the sky just in case Gerry might still come over. But sometimes we did to frighten the girls. The air raid Warden shouted at us "put that ©!!?£ light out.

THERE'S STILL A WAR ON!"

Life went on. After harvest we helped Tredgett to glean the fields for ears of wheat as food for the chickens.

I did not mind queuing at the Co-op. The shop had a super overhead system for carrying money to the cashier from all of the different counters. The pot was unscrewed, the money put into it, the pot screwed up and with a pull of the handle whizzzzed to where the cashier collected

Mum sometimes took us to the pictures where we saw the war carrying on and Disney cartoons. I loved Laurel and Hardy, who were very funny and cowboy films, especially those in Technicolour. When we played cowboys and Indians, I did not mind being an Indian - they seemed very brave to me. My least favourite character was called Old Mother Riley; she was really awful. Mum also let us see the horrors of the German concentration camps on the British Gaumont News →

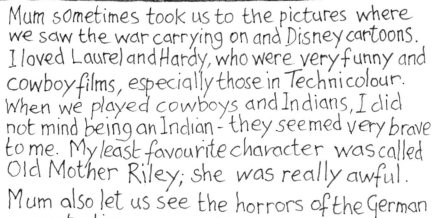

e sent it back with change - Whizz clunk.

SO THAT WE WOULD NEVER LET IT HAPPEN AGAIN.

Then the Germans surrendered. It was V'E' DAY and we went to the Market Square to celebrate the war being over in Europe. We all had to do the hokey-co but Mum said best not in case I got squashed, so a soldier put me on his shoulders and let me hold on to his ears.

When the Americans dropped two atom bombs on Japan, the first on Hiroshima the second on Nagasaki, the Japanese surrendered and

THE WAR WAS OVER

But after seeing what the doodlebugs did to London, I felt very sorry for the Japanese children. Nothing seemed to change. There was still rationing and Daddy still wasn't home

e Americans invited us to a farewell party at the airfield. They gave us lots to eat,
us sit in their Mustangs and pretend to fly them. I thought the belly tanks would
make good boats.

n they all went home and some of the air fields began
e farm land again. We missed them and cannot thank
n enough for what they did. Our town made a memorial
to those who could not go home.

Some girls became GI
brides and went to live
happily ever after in the USA.

On election day a big car came to take Tredgett to the
polling station but she did not go in it. She picked us two
red roses saying "Come, boy Brian we'm going to vote for
Mr. Attlee" and we walked the mile into town.

I don't think Mr. Churchill
was pleased with her.

Not long afterwards the
telegram boy came!

The telegram said, 'ARRIVING STATION 2PM ALL MY LOVE W' and he did, to one of the biggest in history. Some people even clapped and I did not even mind two boys from my school seeing me kiss him, because he was my Daddy and

HE WAS SAFELY HOME